SHOW ME MY MONEY
GUIDE TO FINANCIAL SUCCESS

CHASE CAUDILL, CFP®

Copyright © 2024 Chase Caudill, CFP®

All rights reserved.

DISCLAIMER

Before we dive into the *SHOW ME My Money Guide to Financial Success*, please be advised:

This content is general, provided for informational purposes only, and should not be construed as specific recommendations or investment advice. Always consult the appropriate financial, legal, and tax professionals before making important decisions. Diversification and asset allocation strategies do not assure profit or protect against loss. Past performance is no guarantee of future results. Investing involves risk. Depending on the types of investments, there may be varying degrees of risk. Investors should be prepared to bear loss, including total loss of principal. Michael Caudill is a registered representative and offers securities through Cambridge Investment Research, Inc., a broker/dealer, member FINRA/SIPC, and advisory services through Cambridge Investment Research Advisors, Inc., a Registered Investment Advisor. Cambridge and Appa Financial are not affiliated.

CONTENTS

	Introduction	1
S	avings and Investing	9
H	ousing Needs	35
O	ther Living Expenses	39
W	ants and Other Debts	47
M	onitoring and Making Adjustments	61
E	liminating Debt	65
	Conclusion	85
	About the Author	87

INTRODUCTION

For years, numerous individuals have promoted some kind of financial scheme, claiming to teach you how to make money quickly, get out of debt, invest in a specific vehicle that will solve all your problems, etc. Something I've noticed about all these talking heads or self-proclaimed financial gurus is that they are in it to make money, so they are only picking something relatively small in the large menu of financial habits you should be doing to put yourself in a better financial situation. I understand why they tend to pick one or two things to promote primarily. They are trying to scale their business to sell you more of their products and services. I've been in the financial services business for over 15 years now. I hear the same questions and see the same results over and over again. People want to know what they can do to retire, how much they should save, where they should invest, what the magic number is, and so on. I have followed other so-called financial experts for years and have come to the same conclusion: none tell you exactly what you should do with your money. There are some very broad suggestions, like living below your means or paying off all your debt and then investing. Some offer more detailed instructions than others. More often than not, it seems they overly restrict how you spend your money. Some may say you shouldn't buy a car unless you can pay cash for it, or some may suggest that you should pay 20% or more down on a house, while others tell you to live so frugally you squeak when you walk. After you read this book, I hope you can walk away from it, implement the guidelines, and live this way for the rest of your life without feeling like you are making sacrifices that make you unhappy. You should look at this as a financial lifestyle guide. This guide will tell you exactly how much to spend on various categories, how to pay off debt, how to invest, and how to still enjoy spending. I am not claiming this is easy. For many, the *SHOW ME My Money Guide* will be a challenge; for others, you may look at it and be able to apply it very easily to your lifestyle. If you can read this book and walk away from it being able to start getting yourself on track financially, you are off to a great start, and this guide has been a huge help for your financial future.

The closest thing I can relate managing personal finances to is health and fitness. When people get out of shape and want to lose weight or be in better health, they know they must do something different than their current routine. Most people don't know what to do or how to do it. Some may turn to the latest diet or exercise routine. If they're serious, they will seek the help of a professional. When you talk to a personal trainer, you will be given a routine of exercises and a dietary plan that is specific to your situation.

More often than not, your trainer will tell you if you follow one and not the other, you will get good results, but you will get much better results if you follow the entire fitness and diet plan. Additionally, if your diet and exercise plans are too restrictive or too difficult, it makes it much harder for you to stick to the plan. This is why so many people end up quitting diets by the second or third month. Your personal finances are the exact same in this respect. You get to a point where you know you are not doing what you need to in order to retire comfortably in the future, or maybe you're not living within your means now and need to get your spending under control. If you choose to listen to the latest financial scheme, you may initially improve one aspect of your finances, but you will see rapidly diminishing returns due to the scheme's restrictiveness or limited effectiveness in other areas. If you're serious, you turn to a professional in your field, which may be your financial advisor, or maybe you will try to seek one. If you're at this point, this book is for you. The *SHOW ME My Money Guide* will help you implement the necessary steps and tools to set yourself up for financial success today and in the future.

Another aspect of personal finances that is hard to overcome for many people is the emotional attachment to money. Some people may have a hard time letting it go, while others may have a hard time keeping it. When looking into your own financial picture, you must identify your weaknesses and emotionally detach from the entire process. It's important to understand that your finances are a means to end, whether that end is living comfortably in retirement, or providing shelter for your family, or paying for your standard of living. Just like a fad diet, if you starve your body of all cravings, you will eventually crash and fall off the diet. The *SHOW ME My Money Guide* has also been built in a way to conquer your cravings in a financially healthy way to make sure you stay on track.

WHAT IS THE *SHOW ME MY MONEY GUIDE*?

The *SHOW ME My Money Guide* is short for the six steps you need to implement into your finances in order to seek financial success. The first four elements of the guide are the four uses you should be utilizing your money for each month that you earn. Those uses are Savings, Housing, Other Living Expenses, and Wants. These four categories are how you should be dividing up the use of your monthly income each month. When we talk about percentages, we will reference those percentages as a percentage of your net income, not gross. This will be very important as we discuss your Savings goals and strategies for retirement. Each of these four categories will be allocated 25% of your net income or take-home pay. Think about splitting your monthly take-home pay into fourths. We will be compartmentalizing your money into these fourths. When you know what your fourth take-home pay is, keep that in your mind. That's how we will allocate your money through the *SHOW ME My Money Guide*. The last two parts of the guide are additional steps on Monitoring your Finances and Eliminating Debt after you've got the first four parts established.

This guide may not completely cover every single scenario, but its flexibility allows you to apply it to your own situation. Once we have outlined the basic principles of how the guide can be applied to you, we will take a more detailed look into how you can adjust the different categories to meet your personal objectives. Life throws you many curve balls and you need to be able to adjust your finances to hit them.

The *SHOW ME My Money Guide* is a comprehensive financial system to help you address almost every aspect of your personal finances that you should need in a simplified version with the flexibility to allow you to have your cheat meals with your money to help you stay on track. You will have to be disciplined, and you will have to monitor regularly, but you can still have fun, too. That's why this guide will work for you when others have failed.

BEFORE WE BEGIN...

Before we get into the *SHOW ME My Money Guide* principles, you need to understand a few concepts and assumptions on which we base the system. When we start to discuss different percentages, we will be talking about your net income, not your gross income. If you are self-employed, or receive 1099's, you will need to take some time to figure out what your net income after taxes will look like to apply the principles accurately in this guide. If you're mainly W-2 income, you should be able to go off of your net take-home pay. The reason I use net income instead of gross is mainly because that's the real money in your pocket you must work with after taxes. Your tax situation can change either due to your income changing or the government changing the tax rates. As you go throughout your life, if you use these principles based on your net income, you can always make it work for you without having to rethink your tax situation.

Something else you need to understand is the differences between discretionary expenses and non-discretionary or necessary expenses. Each month, you have costs that you have to pay to maintain your basic needs, which are considered non-discretionary. That includes housing, utilities, food, clothes, insurance, etc. These are expenses that should have priority to be paid each month. Other items that could be included in the non-discretionary expenses are fixed installment payments, student loans, or child support. Discretionary expenses are things that you don't need, but they usually provide a level of enjoyment, like vacations, shopping, entertainment, specialty coffee, etc. It's important to categorize your expenses into these two different categories because if you know what you have to pay for each month to live on, then you can know where you can cut back if you had to on the discretionary items.

It's also important to note that just because an item may fit in a non-discretionary category, it isn't necessarily a non-discretionary item. Take clothes for example: if you buy a $500 brand name outfit, that would still be a discretionary item. As we go through this guide, you will have to distinguish between items that are necessary and items that are not necessary.

Before you dive into the main principles we are about to discuss, a good exercise would be for you to take the last three months' bank statements and/or credit card statements and begin categorizing everything as discretionary and necessary. Total these amounts up for each month. This will help you tremendously when we get into the Other Living Expense and Wants principles of the plan. You should also have all your debt payments and balances that you owe on those debts, as well as the interest rate written down to help when we get to the corresponding principles in the guide. An Excel spreadsheet makes the preparation much easier. You can make adjustments as you need for certain items. Once this exercise is completed, you are ready to start with the four principles of the *SHOW ME My Money Guide*.

$ SHOW ME TIP $

For those that give money to charity or to their religious organizations, I would give this money before you calculate your net income. Whatever your gross income, less taxes and less tithing, that's where you should start calculating your net income each month for your budget. The reason I say to calculate this before you calculate your net income is because it can vary so drastically from person to person. I'm not going to try to tell you how much you should or shouldn't give to those organizations. That's completely up to the individual. If you choose to give a significant amount of your income to these causes, you will have to adjust your lifestyle accordingly. People that have a giving mindset tend not to have issues being more frugal in their other spending.

Sample Spreadsheet: Necessary/Discretionary Expenses

Necessary		Discretionary	
Mortgage/Rent	$ 1,000.00	Eating Out	$ 300.00
Gas/Electric	$ 200.00	Entertainment	$ 225.00
Water/Sewer	$ 40.00	Subscriptions	$ 120.00
Food	$ 500.00	Cell Phone	$ 140.00
Insurance	$ 100.00	Coffee	$ 50.00
Total	$ 1,840.00		$ 835.00

SAVINGS AND INVESTING

The first principle in the *SHOW Me My Money Guide* we will discuss is Savings and Investing. This is the most critical aspect of how you manage your finances and set your future self up for financial success. Before you can truly start investing your savings, you must make sure you have your safety net in place. Your safety net should be an emergency fund. That emergency fund is where you will tap into if you run into an unexpected expense. Those unexpected expenses may be a repair to your house that insurance does not cover, a repair to your vehicle, or maybe an unexpected health care cost. How do you know how much to put in your emergency fund? It depends on your household makeup. Do you have a one-earner household or a two-earner household? If you have a one-earner household, the impact on your family's financial situation is affected significantly more if that earner were to lose their job. The rule of thumb for one-earner households is to make sure you have a minimum of six months of non-discretionary or necessary expenses, with a more comfortable amount of up to 12 months. I will discuss necessary expenses further in the Housing, Other Living Expenses, and Debts and Other Wants principles. These are things you have to pay in order to live on a daily basis and maintain a good credit history. If you are a two-earner household, there is less likelihood that both of you would lose your jobs in the same time frame, but it could happen. Especially if you happened to work for the same company or in the same industry. The rule of thumb for two-earner households is to have a minimum of three months of necessary expenses in your emergency fund, although I highly recommend six months for maximum financial security.

Let's talk about how we will get this money and where this money will be kept. You should know by now what one-fourth or 25% of your monthly net income looks like. If you don't have an emergency fund in place currently, you should devote all 25% of the savings portion of your net income to the emergency fund until you get to the minimum amount you need for your household. Again, that's three months for a two-earner household and six months for a one-earner household. It may take you six months to a year to get this saved up, but this is absolutely necessary to make sure you do not fall into financial ruin in the future. You should place this money in a separate bank account you can easily access whenever necessary, but it doesn't need to be in the same account you have all your other expenses deducted. This helps to make sure you aren't tempted to use the money on those Wants. As far as what kind of bank account, it really doesn't matter as long as you can get the money easily in case of emergencies. If you can, keep it in a higher yielding money market account so you can earn some money on it while it is sitting in the account. Don't get too hung up on what this money returns. The use of these funds is for emergencies. That's how you should be looking at all aspects of your funds. What is the use for these funds? If you can understand money is a means to an end and detach yourself emotionally from its value, you will achieve financial success much easier.

Once you get the minimum three or six months of your emergency fund established, you can back off the amount of your savings to the emergency fund. Now, we're going to redirect the savings that were going to an emergency fund and apply it towards investing. Out of the 25% you are allocating towards Savings and Investing, we are going to split it up into two categories. Fifteen percent will now go towards your Core Portfolio, which is your main retirement account(s), and 10% will go towards Fun Investing. When we start talking about investing, there are two aspects you must understand. The first is the retirement vehicle or type of account, and the next is the investment option within the type of account.

DOLLAR COST AVERAGING

You may have heard the phrase dollar cost averaging before in terms of investing. Dollar cost averaging is what you should be doing with all of your savings and investing strategies. It's basically where you buy into your investment in intervals automatically whether or not the market is up or down. You set your amount and where you want it invested on auto pilot. By setting your investments upon autopilot you are eliminating the emotions of whether to buy now or wait. As we've discussed previously, money is very emotional. What happens more often than not, if left to individuals' choices on when to buy or sell, they will do it at the wrong time, costing them tons of money in the future. Dollar cost averaging will buy when the market is up, down, or flat. Over time, you are averaging your purchases when the market is up, down, or flat, so your return will average out over time. Most employer-sponsored plans are set up this way when the money comes out of your paycheck each month. For your other investment accounts you set up outside of your employer-sponsored plan, you need to set them up this way also. However much you designate towards that account, set it up to be automatically withdrawn from your bank account and automatically invested. This will help you meet your investment goals much more easily over time.

THE CORE PORTFOLIO

We're going to discuss the retirement accounts you should be allocating the 15% of your funds towards to start. Most companies offer some sort of retirement plan to their employees. This may be called a 401K, SIMPLE IRA, 403b, or 457 account. Don't get hung up on the type of retirement plan your company sponsors; they all typically work the same from your standpoint. You typically have a percentage of your income withheld from your paycheck, and they typically match up to a certain percentage of what you contribute as an employee. For example, if you make $1,000 a payroll and have the company withhold 4% of your payroll, which is $40, then the company will give you 4% or $40 in addition to your contribution. Different plans have different stipulations or requirements you must meet before you are eligible to contribute. It typically has to do with being with the company for so many months or years, but that's something you must ask the plan sponsor at your company to be sure when you would be eligible. Once you are eligible to contribute to your company-sponsored plan, your first step is to contribute up to the maximum amount to get the maximum match. For instance, the company may match 100% up to 4%. Like the example above, you put in 4% of your paycheck, and they put in 4%. The 4% match is free money for you. If you don't do the most to get the maximum match, you are leaving money on the table. The next thing I want you to check on with your company-sponsored retirement plan is whether they offer a ROTH option for your contribution. The ROTH option allows you to put your contributions in after tax. The way a ROTH option works is the money goes into the plan after taxes, it grows tax-deferred, and when you meet the rules for the plan, you can take the money out tax-free. This eliminates the need to guess what your taxes may be in the future. If the company doesn't have a ROTH option in the plan, then you can still put in the maximum to get the match. Then, it's time to look at a different vehicle.

> ## $ SHOW ME TIP $
>
> Some people may wonder if you count your employer match towards your savings percentage of the Core Portfolio because that is a percentage going towards your savings, even though your employer is putting it in instead of you. The SHOW ME guidelines for employer matches will be to count half of the match towards your 15% that goes into your Core Portfolio. If your employer matches up to 4%, you can allow 2% to go towards your 15%. The reasoning for only counting half is twofold. First, your employer plan may have a vesting schedule that means you technically don't own all of the match for so many years. If you were to leave the company, you would get all your money but maybe only a portion of your match. Second, most employer matches are pre-tax, which means they will be taxed in the future. We are trying to build as much tax-free savings as we possibly can. By only counting half of it, you are discounting it for future taxes. While, hopefully, taxes will not be 50% for you, this gives you more of a buffer in your savings.

Let's say you are contributing your max in your company-sponsored plan. Now it's time to move on to the next vehicle we want to allocate your savings. The next retirement account we want to set up is a ROTH IRA. Similar to a ROTH option in your company-sponsored plan, the money you contribute will go in after taxes, it will grow tax-deferred, and if you meet the requirements of the ROTH

IRA, when you are 59 ½, you can access those funds tax-free. There is a limit you are allowed to contribute to each year. Typically, that limit increases somewhat each year or so. You just have to look up the maximum for the year you are making that contribution. If you can, contribute the maximum to the ROTH IRA each year. You should check with your financial advisor and/or accountant to make sure you are eligible to contribute to the ROTH IRA since there are some income restrictions if you make over a certain amount of income. That seems to change each year, so you just have to keep a check on those numbers. If you do not qualify for the ROTH IRA, but you have a ROTH option in your company-sponsored retirement plan, you can increase your contribution in the company plan up to a total of 15% of your net income.

There is one exception to choosing the traditional contribution option over the ROTH option. If you are a higher income earner, you can choose to contribute before taxes to your company-sponsored retirement plan. I would suggest if your combined income tax bracket is 25% or more, you would benefit by doing the traditional or before-tax option to save 25% plus on taxes. You can then take that 25% or more of your tax savings and invest it in other vehicles to help you grow your retirement funds. You are not eliminating your future tax liability, but you are getting more money to work for you today.

Before we move on to the next step in the savings principle of the guide, let's talk about the investing aspect of your company-sponsored retirement plan and/or your ROTH IRA options. When you become eligible for your company-sponsored retirement plan, you are presented with several investment options to choose for your money to be invested. These funds are typically mutual funds or exchange-traded funds. If you're someone who likes to do research on investments or funds and choose the ones that you like, then you are more than welcome to do so. For the most part, not very many people fall into that category. We're going to focus on the other options that would apply to the majority of people. When you look through your list of options, you will likely see several options for a Target Date or Retirement Date in the fund. These target date funds are mutual funds or exchange-traded funds that use future dates as the time horizon you are targeting to retire, which will allocate your funds for you based on the date you choose. For instance, if you are 30 years old today, your target retirement age will be somewhere around 35-37 years in the future from today's calendar year. Most target date funds are typically set up on five-year increments, so you would choose 35-40 years in the future if you are 30 years old. Based on the year you choose, the fund will allocate a certain amount to stocks and a certain amount to bonds. The farther away you are from the date of the fund, the more the fund will allocate towards stocks. Since you have a longer time horizon, you need to be in more growth-oriented investments. An important feature of target date funds is they re-allocate the mix of stocks and bonds as you get closer to your retirement age. It's kind of like autopilot: you choose when you plan on retiring, and it will make changes to the allocation for you. These target date funds are a great option for those who do not want to monitor their allocation in their company-sponsored retirement plan and/or their IRA.

Another option that is a perfectly good choice for your retirement accounts is Asset Allocation Funds. Asset Allocation Funds or Style Funds are mutual funds or exchange-traded funds that are focused on a certain mix of stocks and bonds they maintain without changing automatically. When you choose an allocation fund, they may have a description in the fund name like Income, Moderate, Growth, Growth and Income, Aggressive Growth, Global Growth, etc. The name of the fund typically tells you the style of the fund or how it is allocated between stocks and bonds. For instance, a Moderate Allocation may be 50-70% stocks and 30-50% bonds. A Growth or Growth and Income Allocation may be 70-90% stocks and 10-30% bonds. Aggressive Growth or Global Growth may be 90-100 % equities and will have more international exposure to their allocation, as well. Allocation funds vary slightly between fund families, so you have to look at their fact sheets or prospectuses to know exactly how they are invested. The nice thing about allocation funds is that they have a mix of stocks and bonds to fit your style. If you're younger and have a lot of time until retirement, you can choose an Aggressive Growth fund and know you will be 90%-100% in stocks. On the flip side, another feature of allocation funds is that you may be comfortable being more aggressive at an older age, so you can choose an aggressive allocation and know how you're invested. Allocation funds are good for those who tend to be more aggressive for their age versus a target date fund because the target date fund may automatically move them to a moderate allocation when they get within five years of retirement when they want to be more aggressive with their retirement account. Allocation funds may be better for those who want a little more control over their investment style.

Those are the main highlights on how these types of funds typically operate. There are some additional things to keep in mind when considering Target Date or Allocation Funds. The Target Date funds sometimes have a slightly higher fund expense due to the funds being actively managed and reallocated by the fund managers. Additionally, I always try to look at the different dates in a fund family series to see how the fund is allocated at different increments so I have an idea of how the fund will be allocated in the future. Some target-date series are more conservative or more aggressive at different points. You still have to do a little homework to make sure the target date fund will fit your investment style as you get closer to retirement. A disadvantage to Allocation-style funds is that you must ensure you understand your risk tolerance and how the fund is allocated to meet your risk tolerance. You may be a 55-year-old who plans on retiring at 67, but you have a fairly high-risk tolerance, so you want to be more growth-focused. Some growth allocations may be closer to a moderate allocation with only 70% stock allocations because that's what a mutual fund company calls that style allocation. In that instance, since you have a higher risk tolerance and want more growth, you would need to choose the Aggressive Growth style in that fund family that is 90% in stocks to get the more aggressive allocation. Additionally, you will also have to make changes in the future as needed when you get closer to retirement because allocation funds don't change their style over time. You would have to change your fund when you get closer to retirement and want to be more conservative.

Another account that can be utilized in your core savings is a vehicle called a health savings account (HSA). This is not something that is available to everyone. In order to open a Health Savings Account, you must have what's considered a High Deductible Health Plan. You need to check with your company's human resources manager who handles benefits or see what the deductible on your health plan is and look up what the minimum deductible is for a high-deductible health plan. The purpose of an HSA is to allow those with a high-deductible health plan to save money in a vehicle and help pay for those deductibles and out-of-pocket expenses. The HSA is very unique from the standpoint the account offers three tax advantages. The contribution is tax-deductible, the money you contribute is tax-deferred, and when you use the funds for qualified health expenses, the distribution is not taxed. As of right now, when you reach 65, you can roll this money over to an IRA. There is an annual contribution limit based on whether you have an individual plan or a family plan. Let's talk about how you can really supercharge your savings for the future with an HSA. If you have a High Deductible Health Plan and you open an HSA through a brokerage company or an advisor, you can actually take the money you contribute to the HSA and invest it in mutual funds or exchange-traded funds. Now, the money you are contributing will grow in the long run. The idea is that instead of using the money in the HSA for qualified expenses, you would just pay those out of pocket and continue to use the HSA as another savings vehicle. Keep in mind that you can always have access to the funds for medical expenses. Those medical expenses can be from prior years, too. If you keep up with your medical expenses over the course of several years, you can withdraw those funds for those expenses. The HSA can be a very powerful tool in your savings strategy if used properly. Keep this account in mind as you are trying to max out your savings each year.

PUTTING IT TO WORK

Now, we need to discuss a few scenarios to pull everything together to help you know where you should be putting your money, depending on your financial situation. The first thing is to make sure you get the maximum match from your employer. After that, you may fall into two different buckets. You'll be eligible to contribute to a ROTH IRA, or you will not be eligible to contribute to a ROTH IRA because you are over the income limits. If you are eligible to contribute to your ROTH IRA, then contribute up to the max for it. If you contribute the maximum to your ROTH IRA and still haven't reached your 15%, then you can continue contributing more to your employer-sponsored retirement plan. If you are under the AGI limit for the ROTH IRA, you will be able to contribute enough to reach your 15%. If you are not eligible for a ROTH IRA, then you can move on to contributing to a Health Savings account if your health insurance plan is eligible for you to have an HSA. If you cannot contribute to an HSA, then you can continue contributing to your Employer-Sponsored Retirement plan up to the maximum to get to 15% of Net Income. If you have maxed out your company-sponsored retirement plan, contributed to your HSA if eligible, and are still under 15% of your net income, you have to move to a taxable brokerage account now to allocate the remainder of your 15%. I want you to stick with a mutual fund or index fund similar to how you invested your company-sponsored retirement funds until you meet the 15% goal of your net income invested. We'll discuss the brokerage account in a little more detail in the next section. I just want you to be aware that if you have maxed out your other accounts and still have not reached 15% of your net income, then you need to divert those funds into this kind of account and invest it the same as your other core portfolio funds either through target date funds or allocation funds. Below is a diagram outlining the flow of your funds you should follow for your core portfolio.

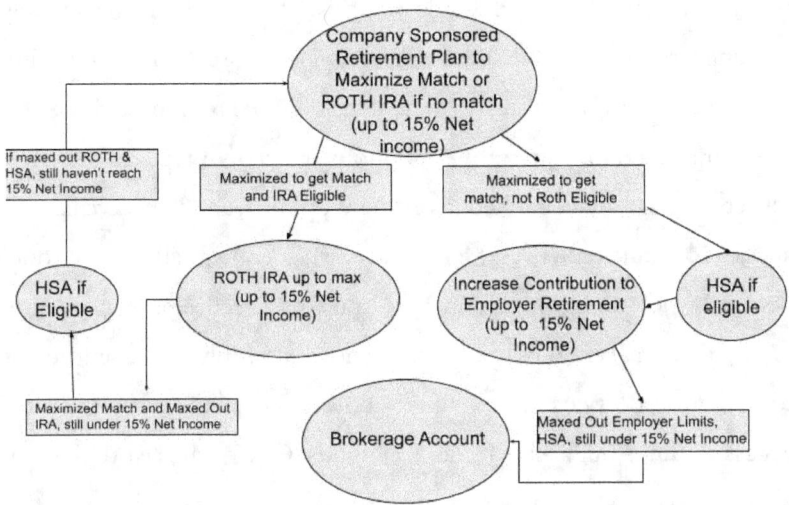

CREATIVE INVESTING

Once you've gotten to where you are saving 15% in a company-sponsored and/or ROTH IRA, we get to the fun part of where you can invest the other 10% of your money. Here's where you can explore some different options you believe best fit your goals or personality. This is the part where you can decide if you want to be a DIY'er or, use a financial professional, or maybe a combination of both. You may want to try to do some DIY investing and seek the help of a financial professional for multiple different vehicles. I'm going to outline some different vehicles and options you may want to choose for this part of your savings and investing budget. Before we dive into the different options, I want to explain why I don't want you throwing all of your money into a company-sponsored retirement plan or ROTH IRA. First of all, I think everyone needs some flexibility in access to funds and diversification in different types of investments outside of basic mutual funds or exchange-traded funds. If you choose to stick with the mutual funds or exchange-traded funds for this portion, there's absolutely nothing wrong with that either. If that's what you're comfortable with, then you will not be wrong in going that way. The reason I believe you need some additional investment options or account types is that your retirement plans have limited investment options, and you have limited access to your funds. As far as access is concerned, you should definitely not touch your company-sponsored retirement plan until after you retire. When I say access, I'm not necessarily discussing access to pay current expenses. I'm talking about access in the future, not just access to funds but access to tax-free funds. One of the last things you want to worry about when you retire is your taxes. Ultimately, this guide is going to hopefully help you get to your retirement goals without having to worry about your taxes. Some people have a goal to retire before they turn 59½, which is typically the age you have to reach before you can take your money out of your company-sponsored retirement plan or your IRA without penalties being applied. If you are wanting to retire early, you will need access to funds that will not be penalized. If you can build a nice fund that isn't taxed either, that's even better. Let's start looking at some options you may want to choose.

$ SHOW ME TIP $

Some people like to use investment calculators to show what-if scenarios that can show you what your future balance may look like if you save so much money a month at a certain rate of return. Sometimes, people tend to be a little too generous on the rate of return they use when calculating these scenarios. I think oftentimes, it's due to their lack of adequate savings, so they try to make themselves feel better by bumping the rate of return up. All we can do is look historically at what the market has returned to gauge what to expect in the future. But remember, past performance is not an indication of future returns. We have another variable that is hard to predict. In the *SHOW ME My Money Guide*, we like to eliminate variables or at least have a bit of a buffer to compensate for the lack of actual numbers. Many people may use a rate of return of 8-10% for their rate of return. While historically, this can be backed up, realistically, this may not be your scenario, especially as you get closer to retirement and your risk is reduced. A more accurate long-term rate range to calculate your returns when running your what-if scenarios would be 6-8%. This gives you room for error if your returns don't necessarily come to fruition in your lifetime. It gives you a slight buffer when calculating your future retirement portfolio balance based on your saving inputs.

WHY IS THIS THE FUN PART OF INVESTING?

This is the part of your plan you can make investment decisions that best suit your interests or behavior. Some people like to do research on different types of investments, and I think you should be able to use your funds to invest in things that interest you. I think it's important that you have the core portfolio you are building in your retirement plans. This part can be where you put your own personal touch on your investing. The first account we'll discuss is just a standard brokerage account. This is a taxable account that has no real tax benefits. You simply put your money into it and choose what you want to invest in. You can choose to open this account online through one of the big-name brokerage firms or you can choose a financial advisor to help make the investments for you. In a brokerage account, you can buy a variety of different products from mutual funds, exchange-traded funds, individual stocks, individual bonds, options, commodities, certificates of deposit, and many others. If you were to work with a financial advisor, they may be able to offer you additional vehicles that we did not list above that you may find attractive for your personal risk tolerance and objectives. You may decide you want to stick with an ETF that tracks the S&P 500. That's perfectly fine, too. None of these options are going to be wrong. You just have to make sure you are comfortable with the risk you are taking. Some people love looking at individual stocks and doing research on them. The only thing I would tell you about individual stocks is I don't want you using this part of your investing budget for day trading. If you're going to buy stocks, plan on owning them for the long term. If you try to day trade, the statistics are going to be against you, and you will likely lose more money than you make. That's the only restriction I would give you if you decided to open a brokerage account and invest in individual stocks. Remember this account does not provide you with any tax benefits, so you must decide if you want investments that create tax liabilities. If you were to buy a mutual fund in this account, they can distribute capital gains each year without your choosing. You may get a 1099 for distributions even though you didn't sell anything because the fund manager sold securities within the fund, which are passed to you. Exchange-traded funds do not distribute capital gains. They provide a more tax-efficient way for you to invest in the brokerage. Also, keep in mind that any fund, individual stock, or security that has a dividend or interest that it pays, you will owe taxes on that as well. Those are just some things to remember if you are concerned about taxes.

Some people have a fascination with precious metals like gold or silver. You can buy or invest in gold and silver in many different ways. You can use your brokerage account to buy an Exchange-Traded Fund that tracks the price of gold, silver, or a group of metals. You can buy stocks in companies that mine for the metals. You can even buy physical gold or silver in bars or coins. Some people enjoy collecting coins. This may be something you find interesting. Gold and Silver, from my standpoint, are mainly for wealth protection. That's how you have to look at it if you buy into these metals. They preserve your purchasing power. They aren't going to give you an income, and they are not likely going to give you a tremendous return, but they should help your money keep up with inflation so you can buy the same basket of goods in the future that you can buy today with the same amount of money. There are pros and cons to owning the ETFs versus physical. Some people have doomsday theories where they think their currency will be worthless one day, so they prefer physical gold or silver. The only negative to it right now is it's not easily converted to cash, but if they're owning it for the purposes of bartering or buying things directly then that's not an issue. It goes back to what your personal objectives and beliefs are that drive you to your investment decisions. If you feel more comfortable owning physical gold or silver, then the comfort that gives you mentally is worth pursuing. I would never tell someone they shouldn't do something if it helped them sleep better at night or made them feel more secure with their finances.

Another popular investment vehicle that is often misunderstood is the use of life insurance products. Most of the time, I hear so-called financial experts talk about life insurance strategies; they seem to make it sound like the silver bullet for retirement. I am by no means claiming anything like this, but there are certain products that could significantly help you in the future. The product that is most widely touted is the indexed universal life policy. There are many working parts of an indexed universal life policy, so it's important if you are interested in this product to seek an advisor who knows how they work and has helped others with them before. The way an indexed universal life policy works is that you have a death benefit for a specified amount for a certain amount of the premium and the remainder of the premium you pay goes to the cash value of the policy. The cash value in the policy can be linked to various different crediting options linked to different types of market indexes. Those crediting options may be linked to the S&P 500 for example. If the S&P 500 goes up for the year, you can make up to a certain amount of that performance, usually called the cap. Let's say the crediting option has a cap of 10%, and the S&P 500 goes up by 15%. You would only make that 10%, not the full

15%. If it went up 7%, you would get 7% since the cap had not been reached. You are typically credited each anniversary of your indexing strategy, which is typically one year but could be more than one year depending on the options available and which one you choose. On the other hand, if the S&P 500 were to lose money on the year, you actually don't lose any money for the year, you just didn't earn a return for the year. This is a very attractive vehicle because you get to participate in the upside to a certain amount, but you don't have to worry about losing any of your money. This is a great strategy for people that are wanting to build a supplemental nest egg to their retirement plan that has the potential to provide tax free income. The money you are putting into the plan is after-tax money, and the growth of the cash value is tax-deferred. When you get to a point where you need access to the funds, you can actually access it in a way where you do not pay any taxes. You can utilize a policy loan on your cash value to access the funds. That loan actually doesn't have to be paid back if you don't want to. Interest is accumulated on it each year. The concept is that your cash value is never withdrawn which means it should continue to grow for a period of time that far outpaces the loans and interest accumulating on your policy. If you have a cash value balance of $500,000 and need $25,000 a year to supplement your social security and retirement plan distributions or income, you can take a loan for the $25,000 each year until you have exhausted your balance. In this scenario, that may last you 20 years or more. How are those policy loans paid, you may ask? When you eventually pass away, they will net the loan balances and the interest from your death benefit. There are a few key points I'm going to highlight if you want this vehicle to work for you. When you choose an indexed universal policy, you must choose a death benefit. There will be some flexibility for you on the premium amount you contribute each month, but there is always a maintenance minimum to keep the policy in force. This minimum will not help you grow cash value; it just pays for the death benefit to stay in force without lapsing. In order for you to grow the cash value, you must over-fund the policy, which means you put in more money than is required, and all that extra goes towards the crediting option that will be linked to a market index. Why aren't we putting all kinds of money into this plan? There is a limit to how much you can contribute to this type of plan called the maximum MEC (modified endowment contract) limit. If you were to contribute more than this amount, then all the money you have put into the plan would become taxable, which is what we are trying to avoid. This amount will vary based on your individual plan characteristics, like the death benefit and how long you plan on paying into the plan. You want to know the maximum amount you can contribute each year and fund up to that amount if possible. The reason I think this type of plan is a very good option for a lot of people is that it helps you grow tax-deferred money and potentially withdraw the value in the future tax-free, which is the ideal situation when you are in retirement, tax-free funds. If you are comfortable with this type of product, you should try to find a financial advisor or life insurance agent who has experience with these types of products and get them to run you some illustrations to find a product that fits your needs.

If you are someone who is familiar with real estate, buying investment properties can be a great option for you as well. I'm not going to go into great depth on real estate in this book because there are books dedicated to helping you figure out how to invest in real estate, and there are so many different models you can use and property types to choose from. If you have knowledge about real estate, are savvy with financing real estate, and/or know a lot about maintaining property, this can be a very good option for you to supplement your overall retirement plan. Real estate provides numerous ways to profit in tax efficient ways. If this is something you would like to consider, please find a good CPA, Attorney, and Insurance agent who can be on your team to help you set it up properly. Just a few words of wisdom coming from someone who invests in real estate personally. Know how to estimate your costs, make sure you have people who can help you manage the property if you can't do it personally, and you have to understand this is a long-term investment like others we have discussed. You will not make a fortune overnight.

In addition to real estate, maybe you are more of an entrepreneur. You might enjoy buying other businesses or starting a business as a side hustle. I encourage anyone who has the entrepreneur itch to get it scratched because if you don't, one day you will always ask yourself, "What if I would have done that?" If you want to use some of your extra savings to explore this option, it could eventually help you ultimately retire. You may be so good at it that you quit your other job and do it full-time. As long as it helps you achieve your personal and financial goals, I don't know how you could go wrong with it. I would make sure whatever you are looking at doing is something you have some experience with and enjoy doing, whatever that business may be. The life of an entrepreneur can be challenging both emotionally and financially. You may decide you just want to own part of another business with someone as an investor and not be involved in the day-to-day operations. That's certainly a possibility, too. Just make sure you understand the risks you are taking with whatever venture you choose.

I would keep it limited to the extra 10% that you're saving, not the full 25% of your monthly savings, and don't jeopardize the 15% you are putting into your core retirement plans.

There are some other options we haven't discussed much, like cryptocurrency or different types of annuities. If you're wanting to do crypto, please be cautious. Don't put in more than you're willing to lose because it can be very volatile. If you're curious about various types of annuities, those are more suited for a conversation with a financial advisor or insurance agent who can go over what best fits your personal needs. There are so many different products that can accomplish many financial objectives that you really need an advisor to help guide you through those decisions.

I've tried to touch on all the topics I could think of that people have ever talked to me about investing in during my career. Hopefully, this has given you some good ideas on what you could look at incorporating into your own investing portfolios outside of the core 15% you are putting in your retirement plans. Maybe you don't really like the idea of doing any of these things we've just discussed in this section; you can always put your extra money into your retirement plan if you want. There's absolutely nothing wrong with doing that, either.

COLLEGE SAVINGS

Something we didn't discuss in the savings chapter was college savings. This is a topic I tend to be torn on. Every family is different, and you and your child must decide whether or not college is the right option. Many parents who went to college themselves like the idea of their children following in their footsteps. There's absolutely nothing right or wrong with thinking this way. However, I think going to college needs to be thought about differently than how most people make their decision. There are many professions that can earn a very attractive wage without having to attend a traditional four-year degree and without having to go into debt to get qualified. I think children should consider their career options much more seriously before making the decision to go to a traditional four-year program and/or grad school. I was fortunate to graduate from college without any student loan debt, largely due to scholarships, but I also worked hard during the summers to help my parents pay tuition. One of the biggest crutches kids have getting out of college is a massive student loan debt. If you want to go into a career that requires a college education, look at the average salaries for that career. Do some calculations on how much you will make versus how much student loan debt you will have. It may not be wise to go to a university that costs $30,000 a year, which leaves you with $120,000 in student loans if you're not going to be making much more than $40,000 a year. You may want to look a little harder at your college of choice or career path. There are many high schools that allow kids to get several hours of college courses before graduating high school. There are several community colleges that offer degrees or programs that are much more affordable than larger universities. Those community colleges usually have agreements with large universities where you may be able to complete two years there and finish at a state university for the same tuition cost as the community college. Maybe you can do a lot of classes online to save yourself room and board expenses. You may have a professional career you are pursuing that requires a four-year degree plus graduate school. Those professions typically pay a higher wage as well. You have to do the math. That's all I am suggesting. Parents and students need to think more seriously about their career path and potential earnings from their career path before they make a decision on how much they will be in debt for college.

Back to how to save for college. I do not think parents should forgo saving for their financial future to pay for their kids' college education. I am not saying you should not help your children pay for college. I am saying you do not need to sacrifice your financial success to pay for your children's college. Do not stop saving your core 15% to pay for it. If you have to use some of the other 10% you save each month to help pay for it, that's ok. You can choose to set up a 529 account for your kids when they are younger if you'd like. This account will grow tax deferred, and your kids can use it for qualified college expenses without paying tax on the growth and without paying a penalty if used for those eligible expenses. If they choose not to go to college, then those funds can be transferred to another child who may go to college, you can give them the funds with a penalty on the earnings, or they may be able to roll it over to a Roth IRA in the future. You could also set them up a UTMA account, which is a Uniform Transfer to Minors Account that will go to them when they reach 18. You do get some tax benefit during their life since the earnings will be taxed at the child's tax bracket. There are no tax deductions or deferrals with this account, but the funds can be used however the owner chooses. If you choose to set these accounts up during your working career, you can choose to use part of the 10% you are saving to go towards these accounts. Here's a creative way to save for college: if you contribute to a ROTH IRA for yourself, you can withdraw those funds in the future for Qualified Education Expenses for your children without a penalty. If they choose not to go to college, or if they were to receive scholarships, your money is still doing what it needs to for you in your ROTH IRA. Another option is if you choose to use some of your 10% in savings above the core amount and put it into a whole life or indexed universal life policy with cash value, you can take a loan on your cash value to help pay for college. You're not taxed on the loan amount, and you don't have to make a monthly payment. Those are two ways you can save for your retirement, but you also have the option to use the funds for your kids' college without being penalized.

RECAP ON INVESTING

Remember to make sure your first 15% of your Net Income that is going towards your Core Portfolio for retirement should be invested in a target date or allocation fund that aligns with your investment goals and time horizon for your retirement age. We discussed how to allocate those funds in employer-sponsored retirement plans, ROTH IRAs, Health Savings Accounts, and possibly Brokerage accounts if needed. The other 10% of your savings can go toward creative investing strategies such as precious metals, real estate, life insurance products, and businesses, or maybe you can keep investing in funds like the first 15%. Remember not to use any of these funds for day trading. Also, keep in mind some of these options require other professionals, such as attorneys, CPAs, Insurance Advisors, and Financial Advisors, to help you. Please make sure to use professionals when you need expertise.

SHOW ME HOUSING NEEDS

A very important aspect of everyone's budget is the roof over your head. Under the housing section of your budget, expenses such as the mortgage payment or rent, the insurance for the house, the taxes for the house, and the utilities to keep the house running are included. For clarification, the utilities that should be calculated for this section should be electric, gas, water, sewer, and trash. Internet, phone, and cable are not necessary for the house to operate and can be more discretionary items or wants rather than necessary. I know everyone thinks the internet and cell phones are necessary, but technically, they are not necessary for your house itself to function and stay maintained; that's why they will be addressed in the Other Living Expense section of your budget.

Before we go any further, I want you to understand that your home should not be considered an investment. Your house, whether you own it or rent it, serves a very important purpose, which is to put a roof over your head and/or your family's. That should be how you look at your housing needs and budget. If you can't afford the kind of house you would like, then find a house to rent that provides the same level of comfort and safety for you and/or your family. Owning a house is not a necessity, and renting is not a bad thing. Everyone's situation is different. It is much more important not to put yourself in financial distress over your housing.

Let's talk a little bit about the differences between renting and owning. With the rising housing costs more recently, buying a home has become a challenge for many buyers, and rents have continued to go up due to several economic factors. What are the pros and cons of renting versus owning? If you rent an apartment or house, you pay the landlord a monthly sum that is agreed upon in the contract you signed before moving in. You are typically responsible for paying all the utilities and maybe a renters insurance policy for your contents. Other than those items, you are typically not responsible for anything else. If something breaks down or tears up, you let the landlord know, and they will send someone to fix it. Usually, the landlord takes care of all the maintenance issues inside and outside of the structure. The landlord also pays the taxes and insurance on the building; however, this does not include your personal contents, which is what the renter's insurance covers. Financially, when you rent you have very little financial responsibilities to be concerned with regarding the property itself. The downside to renting is that you are not paying on a mortgage to build equity in the property, which increases your net worth and ultimately leads to owning the property outright. Additionally, your rent can go up each year after the lease expires. You may have to combat the rising cost of rent, whereas with a fixed-rate mortgage, you would always have the same payment throughout the life of the mortgage. With owning the property you have to pay the mortgage, taxes, and insurance, as well as all the utilities. Plus, you must deal with the unexpected repair or maintenance costs arising from being the owner. You ultimately are building equity in the house; the property should increase each year in value, and you will eventually own it for free and clear. It just depends on your situation, but renting may not be as bad as people make it out to be. It also depends on your priorities and goals. Maybe you rent for a while until you have enough saved up for the down payment on the house. If you have a job that requires you to move often, renting may be the better option. Maybe you work remotely often, so renting could be the best option. Owning a home may not be right for everyone, just like renting may not be right for everyone. These are personal choices you have to make when deciding your own housing situation. The goal for budgeting purposes is to make sure no matter which one you choose, you stay within your desired budget guidelines to set yourself up for success.

The total cost for your housing should be budgeted at 25% of your net income to provide you and/or your family their needed shelter. Before anyone starts to panic, it is possible for your housing to be over this percentage, but that will be addressed in one of the other principles of the guide. If you are currently in a situation where your housing expenses we listed above are over the 25% threshold, it's ok. You are not in jeopardy of financial failure; you just need to know how to address it and categorize it for your budget. If you are currently renting and looking to buy, or if you are looking to rent for the first time, you have the opportunity right now to make this work for you. I am referring to this section as your necessary housing needs. That means you are allocating one-fourth of your net income to the necessary housing situation to live within your basic budget. If you find yourself looking at places to rent or houses to buy that are outside of your basic housing budget, then you are likely stretching your budget a little too far and could possibly be living a little above your means. Again, it's not that you cannot proceed with renting or buying your desired location; you just have to understand how it affects you, which we will discuss later. Another good reason to keep your housing budget under 25% is that you should have no issue with the finance company getting approved for the property you buy. The housing section of your budget isn't too complicated, so we don't have nearly as much to say in this section as we did in the Saving and Investing section. Let's move on to the next part of your budget, the Other Living Expenses.

 OTHER LIVING EXPENSES

This section of your budget will address all of the non-discretionary items in your budget or necessary expenses. Non-discretionary is a financial planning term that I'm not fond of, so I refer to it as necessities or needs. These are things you have to have on a regular basis in order to live your life. Again, the magic number for your necessities should be 25% of your net income. Some people have a hard time distinguishing between wants and needs. In my opinion, needs are expenses you need in order to function in the present society you are living in. We can break those down into basic needs and functional needs.

In general, your basic needs are food, water, air, clothes, and shelter. We already addressed shelter in the Housing section of your budget. That leaves food, water, clothing, and air. Air is readily abundant and free at the current point in time. Who knows, there may be a time when we have to pay a tax or fee to breathe air in the future, but currently that is not an issue. Now, we're down to food, water, and clothing.

Let's go through your food and water expenses first. Luckily, water is readily available, so whether you want bottled water, filtered water, or tap water, that's a very minuscule amount of your budget, so there's not much to be said for water. For this category of your budget, food that is necessary should be the food you buy at a grocery store to prepare at your house. If you eat out, you should reserve that for a Want that will be covered in that section. The reason we are making this distinction is that it is much more cost-efficient to prepare your food at home versus eating out and that food you can prepare at home is healthier for you typically than the food you would get in a fast-food restaurant or other types of dining establishment. Eating healthier food that is more cost-efficient should be considered a need. You're helping your wallet and your health. If you did your exercise before getting into the four sections of your budget, you should have a good idea of what you are spending on food each month already.

Now, we can address clothing, which may be hard for many people to distinguish between wants and needs. For the purpose of distinguishing what is a need in clothing for this section of your budget, it should be reasonably priced clothing for the cultural environment you live and work. For instance, if you are required to wear suits to work, you can easily find suits under $250. I've actually bought some online before for $70 that were more than sufficient for what I needed. However, if you spent $1,000 or more on a suit because you liked it or thought it made you feel better, that would be a want. Let's look at jeans. I can find jeans that I like for $25-30 a pair, so for me, that is my baseline. If I were to spend $75 or $100 on a pair, then I would categorize that as a want. There is some flexibility in the clothing area of this section because it can be so different for everyone. You will have to make the distinction on the baseline for what you consider reasonable and what is a want. As long as you stay within your guidelines, it's not a problem.

Let's look at what would be considered functional needs. These are needs that you must have in order to perform your work duties or be able to function efficiently in society. In today's society, things like transportation, the internet, and cell phones can be a necessity for most jobs now. In the past, the internet and cell phones might be considered wants, but in the present day, they are likely a need for you to function on a regular basis. Internet and cell phones are very affordable now, as long as you don't spend a ridiculous amount on the cell phones themselves. Regarding transportation, this is probably one of the hardest things for people to distinguish between a want and a need. Depending on where you live, if you have some kind of public transportation like a bus or subway, I would consider this to be a need. If you want to have a vehicle of your own to transport you to or from work and other places to run your errands, then we have to get a baseline established. A vehicle should be able to get you and your family safely and efficiently to the destinations needed on a regular basis, such as school, work, grocery store, doctors, etc. The keywords here are safety and efficiency. We didn't say with heated seats, a 20-inch LED display, and all the other bells and whistles they put on vehicles now. If you have a family of four or less, you have several options to choose from. There are large sedans or small SUVs that you can purchase that will both provide you with safety and good gas mileage. If you have a family of five or more, then you have to look at a van or larger SUV in order to safely accommodate everyone. For your budget, we want to allocate 5% towards your vehicle in this section. You should always have some kind of downpayment on a vehicle. If you can't pay for that vehicle outright and you have to finance it, then you need to account for the loan payment on that vehicle up to 5% in this section. If you do the math and realize you'd like to have a little nicer vehicle, that's ok too. We just have to account for it. We will get to that in the next section of your budget. Ideally, you should try to keep the cost of your vehicle or vehicles at 5% of your net income for the Other Living Expenses portion. In addition to your vehicle loan amount, you need to also remember to account for the gas you need to operate your vehicle on a regular basis. The only way to gauge this is to look at your monthly statements and get an average over a three-month period.

If you prepare ahead of time to purchase this vehicle, you can look at taking 5-10% from your monthly savings, still keeping the 15% intact going into your core retirement plans and saving that money for up to 12 months to go towards buying your vehicle. I would only pause investing the 10% for a year or less either until you have enough money to buy the vehicle outright or enough to pay down on the vehicle so the monthly loan payment keeps you within your budget. Don't try to extend reallocating that 10% any further than 12 months because then you will hurt yourself by not investing that money. Vehicles can be tough because some people really like having new vehicles, and others don't care nearly as much. Remember, if you have two earners in the household, you will likely need two vehicles to get each of you to your designated places of work. As far as having a vehicle for your youthful drivers, that will be something I consider a Want. They do not have to have a vehicle to get them to school; you've been taking them for years. Just because they get their license doesn't mean they must have their own vehicle. This is another concept that is difficult for people to take in as well. I'm not saying you can't get them one, but you definitely don't need to consider it necessary for budgeting purposes.

Another necessity in today's society is insurance. Your homeowners or renters' insurance is covered under the housing section, but the insurance for this section will revolve around automobile, health, and life insurance. One thing I want to reiterate in this section, a lot of people think they should always be looking for cheaper insurance, and sometimes, they try to skimp on their coverage to get their rates lower. The problem with doing this is that it could put you in a much worse condition than having the proper coverage. Insurance is supposed to help protect you from unexpected losses, especially catastrophic losses. As you are trying to manage your monthly household expenses, the last thing you need is to have a major loss, and your insurance doesn't cover it properly because you tried to save a few dollars a month. When it comes to all of your insurance coverages, please make sure to choose the right coverages at an affordable rate.

As far as auto insurance is concerned, every state has slightly different coverages, so we won't dive too deep into the specific coverages. However, I will make a few suggestions. On your bodily injury amounts, you need to have at least enough to cover all of your assets. This is a good rule of thumb because if you were to be in an automobile accident and cause serious injury to someone, you have enough coverage for their injuries up to the amount of your assets. If you have some sizable assets, including your home, you should consider adding a personal umbrella to provide even more coverage. The idea is to provide enough coverage through your insurance policies to cover all the injuries and expenses to the injured party so that if they do sue you, they will not try to go after your personal assets. The other coverage you need to ensure you have in place if you have a 10-year or newer vehicle is comprehensive and includes collision. This covers the damage to your vehicle if you hit another vehicle or something hits yours. There is typically a deductible that goes along with these coverages, which is the amount you are responsible for in the event of damage. This can be $250, $500, $1,000, or even more. While having a higher deductible helps reduce the monthly premium, remember you have to foot that deductible if you have to turn a claim in. Make sure you have the funds readily available, which you should in your emergency fund if it is funded properly. Also, remember that the more expensive the vehicles, the higher the insurance premiums typically. Just a side note: when you are trying to pick your vehicle out, you need to consider the insurance premium, too.

Health insurance is something that may be considered in your work benefits that comes out pre-tax. Some companies pay for so much of their employees' premiums, so I would only consider the part of the health coverage you have to pay for in this part of your budget. Health coverage can vary drastically in the coverage. The most important thing to consider is the deductible. In case of a major expense, can you afford the deductible and maximum out-of-pocket expenses with your plan? If you're young, healthy, and don't have any children, then having a high-deductible health plan is usually worth considering. If you have a young family or are expecting a child soon, or maybe you have some health issues, you should try to stick with a plan where you can manage the expenses more easily without having to worry about a large out-of-pocket max or a high deductible. In addition to your health insurance, you may also have dental and vision premiums that need to be accounted for under health insurance as well.

Life insurance is something a lot of people tend to put off and don't think of as a necessity. I am including term life insurance as necessary in your budget because it helps protect your family from financial devastation. At a minimum, you should have enough term life insurance coverage to last you to the age of 60 to pay off all of your debts. Ideally, you should have an additional amount to replace your income. A good rule of thumb is to consider $1 million in term life coverage for every $50,000 of income per year you earn. Again, this should be something in place through the age of 60 at least. Why 60? We'll explain this in more detail later in the Eliminating Debt section. In short, you should have no major debts by the time you reach 60, and your kids should be grown, and out of your household, so you shouldn't have to worry about supporting them now. Also, you should be at a point where you have enough saved for retirement, your surviving spouse should have a good-sized retirement portfolio she can live on. Is it wrong to have your term life beyond the age of 60? Absolutely not. If you want to keep it as long as you can afford it, then you're more than welcome to keep it in place. There are additional life policies that you should consider, but they don't need to be accounted for in this section of your budget. That pretty much covers the basics on the life insurance for your Other Living Expenses section.

SHOW ME WANTS AND OTHER DEBTS

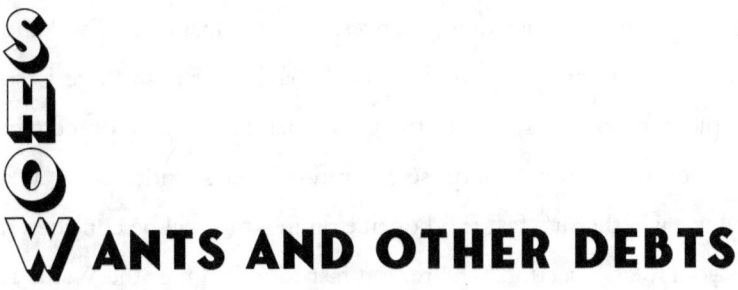

Here's where we discuss the fun part of your budget, the Wants. Before we start, I want to reiterate a philosophy I mentioned earlier in the book. I firmly believe that if you are too restrictive on your spending and your budget, you will likely fail at managing your finances. The fad diet is usually a fad for a reason: it's too hard for people to maintain because they have denied themselves foods they enjoy. It's important to remember moderation is key. Let's start looking at some general categories in this section that people like to spend money on. We will be allocating 25% of your net income to wants. That may sound like a lot, but I will explain why as we get into some of the details.

EATING OUT

Everyone likes to enjoy a nice dinner at a restaurant. Maybe you like to go with your significant other or take your kids to a fun place for them to eat and play games. Food is one of the hardest things for people to control besides their finances. In many instances, food and money can be highly correlated in our behavior because there is so much pleasure in eating certain things or spending money on certain things. For your budget purposes, any time you spend money at a restaurant, whether it's fast food or fine dining, this will be considered under your Wants section. The reason fast food is under the Wants is because you can eat healthier and cheaper if you choose to be prepared and have meals and snacks from the grocery store. Fast food may be cheaper sometimes, but it's never healthier. For it to be considered under the necessities, it must be better for your health and wallet. If you choose to eat fast food, it's a want because you are sacrificing health for speed or taste. If you are choosing to go to a nicer restaurant where you go in and sit down, then you are definitely paying more for your meal than if you were to cook yourself. It's pretty obvious that sit-down restaurants are Wants. Let me be clear: I'm not saying you can't eat at any of these restaurants. We are simply outlining why they are accounted for under the Wants portion of your budget instead of the necessities. If you want a fast-food burger, that's your choice. If you want a nice filet mignon, that's your choice. Just make sure you count your spending for food spent at restaurants under the Wants section.

ENTERTAINMENT

This can be different for so many people. Everyone has different hobbies and levels of entertainment. Some basic things that would be considered under this section are your monthly subscriptions to streaming services, your cable bill, video gaming subscriptions, music subscriptions, and basically any other type of subscription you may be getting charged a monthly fee for. Typically, these subscriptions are not a significant dollar amount, but if you have a lot of different subscriptions, it can run into some money. Ensure you keep up with these and account for them under the Wants section. Other forms of entertainment may not always be each month. Some people like to go to sporting events or concerts. You may not have to account for these each month, but you do so many times yearly that you attend these events. You can average their cost throughout the year, or you can choose to have a lump sum each month you can choose to allocate towards those events.

VACATION

Some of you may consider vacations a necessity, and I do agree with you to an extent. Everyone does need a break to recharge from their careers occasionally. Again, for budgeting purposes, when you choose to spend money on vacations, those should be allocated under the Wants section of your budget. Vacations are typically not every month, so you may not have money you spend each month on them, but you can budget for how much you want to spend for the year on your vacation and allocate it each month. Each month if you don't use that money, it will carry forward until you allocate it for your actual trip. I don't really have any limitations I think you should put on vacations, just that you set a budget for yourself and don't spend more than you allocate towards vacations.

OTHER DISCRETIONARY ITEMS

Any other items that you would not consider a necessity should also be listed in this section. This may include expensive gadgets, name-brand clothing, fancy accessories, etc. This can vary depending on your likes, habits, and hobbies. There are no real guidelines for these items. Just monitor and make sure you are staying within 25% of your Wants.

OTHER DEBTS

We've discussed Mortgages and Vehicle loans in some of the other sections. If you have any other personal debts, this is something I think you should put under this section. Basically, any other personal debt will be a Want for budget purposes. If you have credit card debt, home equity lines of credit, or other secured or unsecured loans, those will fall under this section. Student loan payments will be included in this section as well. Why student loans? As I try to evaluate all aspects of expenses people have, it is my understanding that student loans are something that may have more of a desire than a need behind them. You technically don't need a college degree to have a successful career in many instances. If you do have a profession that requires you to get a degree, remember you are choosing to go into that profession, which is a desire or want. In that respect, that is why I consider student loans to be a Want for your budget. It's important that you keep track of all of your debts on a regular basis, even monthly. I have put together a sample below that you can utilize, or you can simply keep up with the monthly balances in your notes on your phone. Whatever method you choose is fine with me, but you need to know your monthly balance, the minimum payment, and the interest rate for each debt you have.

We'll discuss in the Eliminating Debt section why you need to do this.

Sample Debt Schedule

Lender	Loan Type	Interest Rate	Monthly Payment	Balance
ABC Bank	Mortgage	4.50%	$1,225	$227,305
XYZ Motors	Auto Loan	2.99%	$349	$23,239
Sallie Mae	Student Loan	deferred	$125	$14,793
CC Card	Credit card	18.99%	$35	$3,742

CREDIT CARDS

While we're discussing discretionary spending and other debts, I want to take some time to discuss the use of credit cards. Most people seem to give credit cards a very bad rap. It's most likely because people tend to misuse them, which is why they have such a bad reputation. If you understand how they work, how to use them, and are disciplined when using them, they can be an extremely powerful tool to help you manage your monthly expenses, improve your credit score, and even earn some extra money.

Credit cards are categorized as a revolving line of credit, which means you are allowed to have access to a certain amount of credit based on your approval from the credit card company that can be used and paid back down. What you put on that line of credit in a 30-day period will then either need to be paid back by the next due date, which is usually 15-20 days after the cycle ends, or you will end up paying a fairly high percentage of interest on the balance that remains. The way this typically works is that at the end of the cycle, which is usually a set day each month, your balance on your credit card is calculated, and a due date of roughly 15-20 days from that date is set for you to make a minimum payment in order to stay in good standing. The minimum payment is usually about 1-2% of the balance on your card. For instance, if you have $2,000 at the end of the cycle on your card, your minimum payment might be $40. If you paid just that $40 by the due date, the remaining $1960 would start collecting interest. Interest rates on credit cards can vary from around 8% up to double digits in the 20+%. Those are high rates you will have to pay on that remaining balance. This is where many people get into trouble. They start only paying the minimum payment. What happens is if you only pay the minimum payment, it will take a very long time to pay that balance back with that high interest rate. Often, people get into more trouble because they may only pay the minimum payment, but then they use their credit line again and add to the balance. Now, they're only paying the minimum payment, getting charged double-digit interest, then adding to the balance that will get charged the double-digit interest. Additionally, at some point, if you are ever late on a payment, there are usually hefty late-pay penalties that get added to that balance as well. This is how things can get out of hand very quickly for many people who don't use credit cards properly. If you are able to keep your balance on your credit card in check or within your budget, and you pay the full balance off each month, you don't owe any interest. Actually, you were able to create a window where you used your credit card on your monthly expenses and were given roughly 15-20 days to pay it off with no interest. If used wisely, credit cards can be a very powerful financial tool.

One of the biggest things credit cards can do for you is build your credit score up if they are used wisely. When I was 18, before I went to college, I applied for a student credit card. I think it only had a $300 limit on it. I would use my credit card only for gas and food. Each month, I would pay it off. I did this all through college. When I graduated college and went to get my first loan, I had a credit score of over 700, which helped me get a much better rate on my loan, and I didn't have to get a co-signer on that loan. Another trick you can do to help your kids out before they're 18 is adding them as an additional signer on your credit card. They don't even have to use the card; just be listed as an additional signer, which lets them piggyback off your credit history from that card. Then, when you think they're ready to start using the card, you can let them try it out for themselves. If credit cards are used wisely, they can be the best credit-building tool for young people right out of the gate. This helps them get started out a step ahead. By already having a good credit score, they will be able to get loans easier, get better rates on loans, be able to put things in their names without a cosigner, and save a ton of money in the loan run.

Rewards are another great perk to using credit cards. There are so many cards to choose from now, but you just have to do some research to see which one would be the best fit for your spending habits. Some offer cash back based on where you spend your money each month. For instance, they may give you 2% back on gas or groceries and 1% back on anything else. Some cards have airline perks that give you flyer miles for your plane tickets. Of course, if you don't travel or fly much, these cards are of no benefit to you. Some cards are themed to be used at specific places or websites. For instance, Amazon has a Prime card that gives you points on anything you spend to be redeemed on your Amazon purchases. If you can use your card wisely and pay the balance off each month, then you actually get rewarded to do so by these credit card companies. I want to offer a quick warning on rewards. Do not spend money just to get rewards. You will end up overspending on things you don't need, and you may put your finances at risk by doing so. Rewards should just be a perk for planned and disciplined spending habits.

Another great benefit of credit cards is the 0% offer. You can find some cards that will offer you 0% for so many months when you sign up for those cards. I think this can be of great benefit when you have a decent-sized purchase you need to make, whether it's a major home repair or a vacation. Basically, you are given a certain number of months to pay it back without any interest being charged. Again, this is a great tool if you use it wisely. Don't go buy a bunch of things you don't need just because you have 0% interest for a while. Use it for bigger ticket items to help you maintain your monthly budget. Even after the initial 0% interest period is over, many of these credit card companies will offer it to you later down the road as a special offer. I get these offers all the time with my cards, and I use them when they come up.

The best way to use credit cards is to know your monthly budget and only put certain types of items in your monthly budget. For instance, use them for groceries, gas, and maybe for your discretionary spending. You should already have a monthly budget for those types of items, so you can keep an eye on how much you're spending as you go through the month. Most cards have a way for you to categorize your spending when you log in to the site or app to help you keep track of where you are spending your money. This may actually be an easier way for you to help monitor your monthly spending. You may also find it better to put items you need more help tracking on the credit card since it is separate from your bank account. Most people tend to set up fixed payments like their rent or mortgage, and car payments from their bank accounts. By using a credit card, you can keep those variable costs separate from your fixed costs to help give you a better idea of where you are spending your money each month.

I just want to reiterate that credit cards are not for everyone. It does take some discipline and planning to use them properly. If you don't have a monthly budget planned out, credit cards may not be a good option for you. If you are trying to get yourself on the right track and are planning your budget, I would practice your budget for a few months first to make sure your numbers are good, then you can look at incorporating credit cards to help you monitor and manage your monthly expenses, plus earn some extra money with those rewards.

OVERAGES ON MORTGAGE OR AUTO LOAN

If you recall from previous chapters, we discussed the baseline for your housing should be 25%, and your auto should be 5%. It is acceptable to go a little over that amount, but you must account for it. If you choose to go over those guidelines, anything over those guidelines up to 5% more for each needs to be accounted for under the wants section. On your housing, the cost from 25-30% should be listed under wants because you are starting to push the limits of going from an affordable house to possibly starting to live outside your means. Therefore, we will categorize that extra 5% as a want. The same thing applies to your vehicle loans. If you want a nicer vehicle, anything from 5-10% of your net income should be accounted for in the wants section of your budget. The reasoning is that you need a safe, dependable vehicle, but you don't need a vehicle that costs 10% of your take-home pay a year.

Something I need to point out as you are trying to decide how you want to spend your money: this section of your budget is where you can really make or break your financial success. Keep in mind that as you set your budget, the more you spend on a house or car, the less you have to spend on other discretionary items. The more you spend on your house or car, the less you may have to put extra in savings. You can actually add to one section of your budget, and that's your savings section. The less you spend on housing, vehicles, and discretionary items, the more you can put into a savings vehicle to invest in your future. I'm not saying you shouldn't spend money on the things you like and enjoy. You just need to be mindful of how your spending can impact your future self. If you stay in the 25% range on housing and the 5% range on a car loan, you might be able to hold your discretionary spending to 20% or even less. Any of that extra can go towards one of two things: investing or eliminating debt. By putting more money into those two things, you are helping yourself be more prepared for financial success one day. It's always a give-and-take with discretionary spending. You can spend money on the things you like, but you are giving something up by doing so. Again, it is healthy to reward yourself, but I'm just reiterating that this is where you can really make some headway in your finances if you choose to.

That concludes the core pillars of your budget: Savings and Investing, Housing Expenses, Other Living Expenses, and Wants and Other Debts. Each with 25% allocation of your net income. The last two parts of the *SHOW ME My Money Guide* are the M and the E. In these chapters, we are going to discuss ways to stay on track, adjustments to make, and steps to take to be financially successful when we reach our desired retirement age.

RECAP - CORE BUDGETING PRINCIPLES
SAVINGS AND INVESTING

Before we move on to the next few chapters, let's take a minute to summarize the core budgeting principles. For your Savings and Investing, you will allocate 25% of your net income to this category. The first thing to establish is the emergency fund with the full 25% until you reach your minimum target of either three or six months of necessary expenses. Remember, 15% will go towards your core retirement fund portfolio in a company-sponsored retirement plan, a ROTH IRA, and/or another option such as a brokerage account if you max those limits out. The other 10% of the savings will go towards other investments we discussed in that section or back into an employer-sponsored plan. That 10% portion of your savings can also be turned on and off for different variations you may have in your budget, such as saving for a vehicle. If you need some extra to pay off your Other Debts or if you have to use some of your emergency funds, you can pause this portion of your savings to replenish or pay off those things but don't do this for more than a consecutive 12-month period.

HOUSING

Your housing costs include your rent and/or mortgage payment, the house insurance, the property taxes, and the utilities required to keep the home itself in good maintenance and operation, which are typically electric, water, sewer, and gas. These expenses should account for 25% of your net income. As we discussed in the Wants section, your housing expenses can run up to 30%, and you will still be able to safely maintain your lifestyle, but you will have to take 5% away from your Wants. Essentially, you are paying a little more for a living situation you want rather than need.

OTHER LIVING EXPENSES

These are primarily your necessities outside of housing. Basic transportation, groceries, food, forms of communication, etc. You should try to keep these expenses under 25% of your net income. This category also includes your vehicle loan payments. As we discussed in this chapter, a vehicle should not take up more than 5% of your net income to provide you with necessary transportation. If you choose to spend a little more on a vehicle, you can spend up to another 5% for a total of 10% of your net income on vehicle loans. That extra 5% needs to come from your Wants or discretionary category because, again, you are choosing to put yourself in this situation, so it will reduce how much you should spend in that category.

WANTS AND OTHER DEBTS

These are the items you choose to spend your money on, the things that make you happy in life. This should be no more than 25% of your net income, as well. If you choose to have a higher housing expense or vehicle loan, this can be dwindled down to 15%. The choice is completely up to you. You have to decide what things will make you happier in life. Maybe it's a nicer home or vehicle for some. It may be more extravagant vacations for others. This is where you have the freedom to spend on whatever you like. Just make sure to keep it under control and never go over the 25% of net income.

CORE PRINCIPLES BUDGET	
Savings & Investing - 25%	**Other Living Expenses - 25%**
Emergency Fund: up to 25% until funded	Food
Retirement Plan & IRA: up to 15%	Clothing
Creative Investing: up to 10%	Insurance
	Auto Loan: up to 5%
Housing - 25%	**Wants 25%**
Mortgage/Rent	Internet/ Cell Phones
Home/Renters Insurance	Entertainment/ Subscriptions
Electric, Gas, Sewer, Water, Trash	Food
Taxes	Vacations
	Housing: >25% and < 30% total
	Auto loan: >5% and <10% total

ONITORING AND MAKING ADJUSTMENTS

Now that we've gone over the core principles of your budget, it's time to put them into practice. Before you started reading the first four core principles of the SHOW ME budget, you should have put together some numbers from your bank statements and/or credit card statements to give you an idea of your current spending habits. Once you have those numbers, you need to see how they line up and see how far off your different categories are to get them under the desired percentages for each core principle. If you are close to being within that core, I would suggest you continue what you are currently doing and monitor your spending each month. It's important to continually monitor your spending behavior each month for a while until you have your habits under control. Even if you do get to a point where you are consistently staying within your guidelines, it's still good practice to continue to monitor your monthly expenditures. I will relate this back to dieting. If you track your calories, protein, carbs, and fat, it is much easier to maintain a healthy weight. If you get comfortable and slack off on tracking, you will likely drift back to your old habits and put that weight back on. Monitoring your monthly spending habits will help lead to longer-term financial success.

Let's talk about what you need to do if your budget is outside of the guidelines of the four core principles. First, you must have your emergency fund established before you can make any major adjustments. Back to the Saving and Investing Principle, save up to 25% of your net income until you have your desired balance in the emergency fund. Once that is done, you need to look to see where you are over your limits. If you are spending more than 25% on housing or more than 30%, with 5% coming from discretionary spending, you may need to look at how to help reduce your housing costs. This may be as simple as shopping for your homeowner's insurance for a better rate or seeing how you can save money on your utilities throughout the year. If the problem results from your mortgage or rent being too high, you may have to make a harder decision. Ultimately, if you are living in a home you are safe, happy, and comfortable with, moving may not be the best solution. You may need to find other areas you need to cut back, namely discretionary spending. If moving is something you could consider, then you may need to sell your home or find a different property to rent once your lease is up. Housing can be one of the hardest things to control if you're already in a situation where your housing to net income is over the desired allotment for your budget. When you look at your necessities, it may be difficult to find much you can cut back on in this section, but you can always be more frugal if you have to be. You can try to shop smarter for your food and other groceries by using coupons or shopping around for better-priced products. The one area of your budget I will tell you to make a drastic move on if you exceed the limit is your vehicle expenses. I think car payments are a major problem with most households. If your car payments are over 10% of your net income, you are spending way too much on your car. Keep in mind vehicles go down in value over time. You're making a large monthly payment on something that will likely not give you your money back when you go to sell it. Even more reason not to have an outrageous car payment. If you're over the limit, you need to sell it and get a more affordable vehicle. That leaves discretionary spending. This is where you likely will need to make most of your adjustments if your budget is outside the guidelines. More often than not, this is where people blow their budgets. Most of the other expenses for housing and necessities don't change much. Your spending on the Wants is where you get in trouble. For expenses, this is the area you will be spending most of your time tweaking as you track your spending throughout the first initial months of your budget.

Spending is not the only thing you should be monitoring. I think it's important for you to keep track of all your debts, savings, and investments. We will discuss how to handle your debts in our next principle, but right now, you should ensure you know the current balance, the interest rate, and the minimum payments you have to make for each debt. By tracking your debts, you are more aware of the balances, making them seem more urgent when you look at them each month. You should also always have a running balance of all your bank accounts, your emergency fund, and your investments. Each month, you should update the current balance for each one of these. You should periodically check your monthly budget totals to make sure you are carrying enough in your emergency fund for your needs. We will discuss some goals for your investment balances in a later chapter. That's why it's important to monitor your balances so you know where you stand as you approach your desired retirement age. If you need to think about adding more to your core portfolio to achieve those goals, then you can try to make some adjustments in other areas of your budget to do so.

Remember, as you go through your budget each month, once you have your core percentages under control, it's okay if your core percentages go over a percent or two every now and then. If they start to go over several months in a row, you should re-evaluate all of your expenditures and try to see where the overages are occurring. What happens if an emergency comes up? That's what you have the emergency fund for. You can tap into your emergency fund if you have any kind of unexpected maintenance for your vehicles, if something in your house tears up that needs fixed or replaced, if you have an unexpected medical expense, or something else of urgency and necessity that must be paid immediately. If you do have to use your emergency fund, I would reallocate up to 10% of your monthly savings to replenish the emergency fund. Once it has been replenished, you can continue saving and investing 10% the same way you did before. I also wouldn't count that emergency against you from your budget standpoint. Your budget is meant to handle your expected monthly costs. Your emergency fund is for the unexpected necessary costs.

SHOW ME ELIMINATING DEBT

This is a concept that can be one of the hardest for people to overcome, especially if they're already in a considerable amount of debt. We're going to talk about ways you can tackle your debts, strategies to implement, and some goals you need to obtain throughout your life with your debt balances to help you make it to financial success. The first thing you need to do is go back to the spreadsheet you should have completed when you first started this book. Look at your debt balances, interest rates, and payments. Put them in order of highest interest rates first. Then, I want you to highlight the highest interest rate balance. Next, I want you to look at your payment amounts. Aside from your mortgage, I want you to highlight the highest monthly payment amount.

HIGHEST INTEREST AND HIGHEST PAYMENT

It's important to get the highest interest rate paid off the soonest, because it saves you a tremendous amount in interest over the life of the loan. Then, if you focus on the highest payment amount next, it will give you more monthly cash flow to either pay off your other debts or invest more. Once you have identified the highest interest debt and the highest payment amount, excluding your mortgage, let's figure out how we can get these paid off. The first thing you should be doing when trying to eliminate your debt is to pay off the highest rates first. Maybe you don't have any double-digit rates, so I would consider anything above 6% to be a higher rate. Whatever your highest interest rate debt is above 6% is what you want to attack first. Remember, the goal is not to have any personal debt outside of a mortgage or a vehicle loan. It doesn't matter if you are within your core limits or not; getting personal debts paid off is important. Once you've identified the personal debt with the highest rate, we need to figure out where we're going to get the money to pay it off within a 12-month period. You have to decide where you want to free up some money to start paying it off. The first thing you can consider is to lighten up on your discretionary spending each month and apply that extra to the debt. Typically, you won't be able to cut back on your living expenses or housing, so the only other place you can redirect money from is your savings. Remember, you should always save 15% of your core portfolio. The extra 10% you should be saving and investing is where you can get some of that extra money from to pay down this debt. Your goal should be for a 12-month turnaround to have the debt paid off. It's okay to redirect that extra 10% in savings for up to 12 months to get it paid off.

Once this is paid off, you should feel a little weight being lifted from your financial shoulders. You should go down your list and choose the next highest interest debt and get a plan to pay it off in 12 months or less. Hopefully, you now have freed up some extra monthly cash flow you were using to pay that debt. You can redirect that money to go towards your next debt. This is often referred to as the snowball method. Once you get one debt paid, use the money you were paying on it each month and apply it to the next debt. You can use this method, but again, I want you to have it paid in 12 months or less. You may still have to utilize some funds from discretionary or savings to accomplish this. I want you to continue to do this until all of your double-digit interest rates are paid off. Once you've gotten all of your double-digit interest rates paid off, or maybe you didn't have any to start with, I want you to focus on the highest payment amount, excluding your mortgage and not including your auto loan, unless the auto loan was double-digit interest. If you have an auto loan that has double-digit interest, it's likely going to fit this description. If you don't have a double-digit auto loan, you can focus on the next highest payment amount. Calculate how much you need to pay each month to get this paid off in 12 months. Hopefully, you have enough extra cash flow now where you paid the other debts off; you don't have to redirect the 10% in savings. The idea behind paying this off is that you can free up even more monthly cash flow to be used for paying off your auto loan and/or adding more to your savings. If you still need to redirect some funds, try to use your discretionary spending to help finish this debt off so you can get that savings back to work for you. This method works well because it gives you a confidence booster up front within the first 12 months, and it helps you free up more monthly cash flow. If there are any other debts left outside of your mortgage or auto loan, you should have no issue paying them off quickly with all the extra money you have each month now.

> **$ SHOW ME TIP $**
>
> When trying to eliminate higher-interest debt, if you have more than one account balance, try to pay off the smaller balance first, even if the interest rate on the small account balance isn't as high as the others. Choosing a smaller account balance first should be easier for you to pay off, and it will give you a confidence boost as soon as you get it paid off. More often than not, that's all you need when trying to control your finances. Sometimes, the confidence boost will help you more than saving a few extra dollars in interest.

AUTO LOAN

Let's talk about those vehicle loans. Just to recap, your auto loan should be no more than 10% of your net income, preferably 5%. If you go over 5%, the amount over 5% up to 10% should be considered discretionary, as discussed in previous chapters. When you talk about your auto loan, no matter if it's 5% or up to 10% of your net income, you should base it off of three years or less. I know there are programs that will let you go up to even 10 years on vehicle loans, but that's for people who are trying to stretch their finances out too far. If you don't have enough down payment to keep your vehicle loan at or below 10% of your net income while being paid off in three years, then you shouldn't buy that vehicle. You are simply buying too much vehicle for your budget. Vehicles can make or break your budget. I know it's nice driving a new vehicle or good-looking car, but it's not worth sacrificing your future financial success to look good in something that goes down in value. That's the guideline you should stick with on a vehicle: no more than 10% of your net income and structured so it can be paid off in three years or less. Once you have your other personal debts paid, as we mentioned above, then you can start to work on getting your vehicle paid off sooner by adding more to your payment from the extra cash flow you freed up.

MORTGAGE

Many people get in their heads that they need to pay off their mortgages. Some people, including some of the so-called financial experts, try to say you should use all the money you can to pay off your mortgage even before investing in your retirement. I think this is completely wrong. I think your mortgage should be the very last thing you pay off. I don't think you should stop investing in your retirement to pay your mortgage off, either. The reasoning is that the money you pay on your home reduces the monthly interest expense as you pay more on the principal. The home value should hold steady and appreciate over time, as well. If you put extra money toward your loan each month, the best you will do is save yourself some interest. I know interest rates have gone up significantly, but I know there are still people who are locked in at 2.50-3.50% rates. Here's an example of what this would look like if you paid extra on your mortgage versus using that extra to invest.

Let's look at a basic example of someone who has bought a $250,000 home. Someone today may have a 30-year fixed mortgage for 3.00%. That's what we will use to set up this example. If someone has a $250,000 mortgage loan that is set up on a 30-year term with a fixed rate of 3.00%, then their monthly payment would be right at $1,054 a month. That does not include any taxes or insurance, strictly the mortgage payment by itself. You can go to any mortgage loan calculator online to get this information. I went to mortgagecalculator.org for these calculations. Now, you are contemplating whether you want to pay extra on your mortgage loan or if you should take that extra money and put it into your retirement savings that would be invested in a diversified mix of stocks and/or bonds. Let's say you want to pay $500.00 extra monthly on your mortgage payment. By doing this, you would cut your mortgage down to be paid off in 17 years and three months with a savings of $59,242.14 in interest. That's a huge savings over time, almost cutting your mortgage term by half. Instead of putting $500 per month into an extra principal payment on your mortgage, let's look at putting that $500 into a retirement account that is invested in the market, and we will assume an average of a 7% return compounded annually. We will also only do this for 17 years since that would have been the length of time your mortgage would have been paid off. If you save $500 a month for the next 17 years at a compound annual rate of 7%, at the end of the 17 years, you would have roughly $190,905.53. You would have put in $102,000 of your own money, and your funds would have grown by roughly $88,950.53. You can find many different investment calculators that will also make these calculations for you. I used calculator.net for the calculation.

Let's take that one step further. After 17 years, let's say you continue to put $500 a month into a retirement vehicle that grows at roughly 7%. At the end of 30 years, which would be the same time you pay your mortgage off, you could have $584,726.30. You would have contributed $180,000 of your own money, which would have grown by

$404,726.30. And now you don't have a mortgage payment and have a nice nest egg built up. Some people may say they want to pay their mortgage off early, and then they'll put more money into their retirement. Let's say you added $500 to your mortgage payment, it was paid off in 17 years, and then you decide you would put $1,000 a month into your retirement vehicle that would grow at the same 7% return over the next 13 years, which is the same time frame as the 30-year mortgage, just to keep all the numbers on the same time levels. By the end of the 13 years, you could have roughly $249,347.14. That's less than half of what you could have had if you would have just done the $500 a month for 30 years.

What if you put $1,500 a month in your retirement vehicle after you paid off your mortgage, since you were paying the $1054 on the payment, plus the $500 extra dollars? At the end of the 13 years, you would have roughly $374,020.71. It's still not anywhere near what you could have had if you had put the $500 a month in the retirement vehicle from the beginning instead of paying extra on the mortgage.

If your interest rate on your mortgage is closer to 7%, then the numbers do get a little less impressive on the savings versus the growth. The thing to remember is if you add money to your investments, they are compounding over time. When you pay down the mortgage, in the end, you are just saving the interest. It's simply a game of can that extra money be worth more than the interest saved over the same amount of time. Then you have to remember, since you saved that interest, what did I do with that money? Did you save it elsewhere? The likely answer is no. You probably just put that extra money into the mortgage and didn't take advantage of the interest you saved to invest it elsewhere. It's quite obvious with some basic calculations that, in the long run, the potential for your retirement is much greater than the mortgage being paid off early. Mortgage interest is also tax deductible if you itemize, so you're potentially not paying nearly as much interest as you might think due to the tax advantage of paying that interest.

With all that said, the only way I want you to consider paying any extra on your mortgage is to have it paid off by the time you are 60 years old or within five years of your desired retirement age. When they are 60, most people are either close to retirement or contemplating retirement in the next five years or so. When you are at or near retirement, it's important that you are completely debt-free. I still don't want you to pay extra on your mortgage until later in life because you should have been putting that extra money into your retirement savings so you can retire at least in your 60s. Once you've got all your other debts paid off, you can look at adding some extra to your mortgage payment when you're 45 or older, with a target to have it paid off by 60 or sooner. All that extra money you could have been paying on your mortgage up until now could have been enjoying compound growth all those years, which would have been far more beneficial in the long run for you. At 45, you can start doing some calculations to see what it would take to have it paid off by the time you reach 60. I still wouldn't think about putting extra money down until you were 50 or older because when you're 45, that money still has 20 years or longer it could be working for you in your retirement account. The only other exception I would make to paying extra on your mortgage is if you are able to save 25% of your net income, you've paid off all of your other debt, and now you want to reallocate those funds to your mortgage to pay it off sooner. I still think if you were to do some numbers, it would benefit you more to put those funds into your savings and investing, but if you're already saving 25%, it may make you feel much more relieved to have your mortgage paid off sooner. At this point, you just have to ask yourself, "What would make me feel better: more retirement money or no mortgage payment?"

To review, if you have consumer debt outside of your mortgage and vehicle loan, you should be trying to get this paid off first using the strategies we discussed. Work on any double-digit interest balances, then move to the highest payment amount. If you have any more after that, keep using the snowball method to pay it off; since you have freed up some extra cash flow, you won't have to sacrifice your savings. As far as the vehicle loan is concerned, if you set it up correctly, you can pay on it so it is paid off in three years or less. This monthly payment should be accounted for in your core budgeting categories. Finally, for your mortgage, pay your regular payments on it to have it paid off by 60 or within five years of retirement. You could potentially use your extra funds from paying down your other debts if that would make you financially happier.

DEBT PAYDOWN ORDER

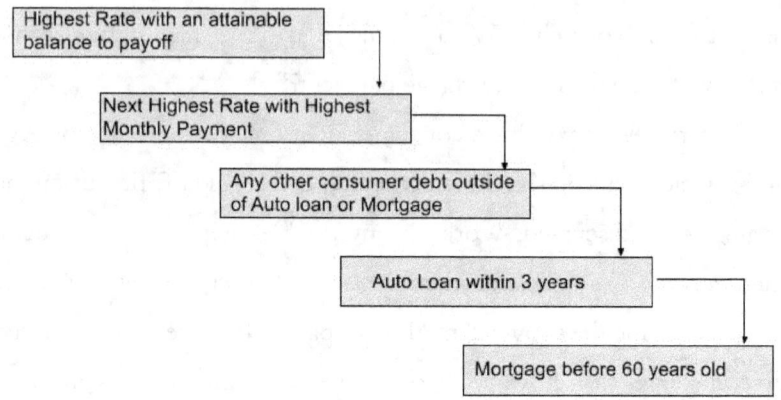

GOALS

Now that we've discussed the core budgeting principles, how to monitor and adjust your budget, and how to eliminate debts, we want to look at some financial goals you should try to accomplish throughout your life. One of the biggest questions people seem to ask is, "What's my retirement number?" Basically, how much do I need to retire and/or when can I retire? In all honesty, this is the crux of why I am writing this book. I see people make so many financial mistakes throughout their lives; if they had had a simple plan in place, they could have known the answer to these questions and set themselves up for financial success. When you go back and look through the process in the core budgeting strategy, we are looking at our after-tax money. So many people try to tell you to budget on your gross. The problem with your gross is the taxes. We have no idea what our taxes will be in the future. They may be the same, more, or less. There's no way of knowing. This is a variable we have to eliminate. I based the SHOW ME My Money budget on after-tax money because that's the real money we must work with. In addition, the investment strategies we incorporated focus on vehicles that will help you grow your retirement funds with the least amount of tax implications, if any. Let's get back to your retirement number.

When you retire, you will no longer need to save 25% of your net income because you should have accumulated enough money to live on by now. Let's take your net income and subtract that 25%. Now, you've got 75% of your net income left. We discussed in the eliminating debt section how you should have no debt, and your mortgage should be paid off by 60 or within five years of when you plan on retiring, whether that age is sooner or later than 65. Looking back at the core budget limits for housing, you should have 25-30% in housing costs. If you eliminate the mortgage, you should free up an additional 20-25% of your net income from housing. So that means 45-50% of your pre-retirement income went towards things you no longer have to pay for. Interesting. That means you are only looking at needing to replace 50-60% of your pre-retirement income for retirement. Now that we look at those numbers, it seems much more attainable than you thought. The one thing you should consider is any increased healthcare costs you may experience in retirement. If you want to retire prior to 65, this is a major consideration because you are not eligible for Medicare until 65. That means you must account for your health care costs out of pocket until you are 65. Once you reach 65, if you choose your healthcare options wisely, your healthcare costs, for the most part, should be very manageable. If you took advantage of a Health Savings account during your lifetime, those funds can help you overcome your healthcare costs in retirement. You should still be able to manage your post-retirement budget with 50-60% of your pre-retirement funds.

Looking at what's left we have to consider paying for in retirement, you have Other Living Expenses, Wants, and some Housing Expenses. This is something I would like to point out as we have gone through the *SHOW ME My Money Guide*. This budget was designed so you shouldn't have to be so frugal you never get to spend any money on things you enjoy. Hopefully, over your lifetime, you will spend money on things you like to do or things that make you happy. I hear people say all the time they wish they had done things when they were younger because when they retire, they may not feel like doing them, or their health may not allow them. Ideally, if you had done this during your lifetime, when you get to retirement, you shouldn't have a pent-up desire to do the things you wished you would have done when you were younger. That said, you may not necessarily need to spend as much on items in the Want section of your budget post-retirement. Back to the 50-60% of your pre-retirement net income. That's what you need to focus on when you think about saving for retirement.

Let's talk about a retirement concept that has long been believed regarding using your retirement funds. It's called the 4% rule. The idea is that you can withdraw up to 4% of your retirement funds each year, which should last 25-30 years. Some years, you may not even have to touch the principal balance. Others, you may have to do so if the return is less than 4% or your costs have risen over time due to inflation. The 4% rule has been the general consensus for years. I don't see a reason not to base your retirement fund number on the 4% rule. As we discuss your retirement number, if you were to retire sooner than 65, you may need to make sure you have some more cushion in your retirement funds since you will likely need your funds to last longer than someone retiring at 65. That said, if you wanted your pre-retirement spending to be maintained, you would need approximately 25 times your pre-retirement spending of 50-60% of your pre-retirement net income. If your pre-retirement net income was $80,000 and you spent $40,000 on your Other living expenses, your Wants, and some Housing Expenses, then you would need $1,000,000 in your retirement funds to consider retiring. At $1,000,000, if you apply the 4% rule, you could draw $40,000 a year. See how all that work you did following your budget and saving can pay off. This budget doesn't just help you save or help you pay off debt. It sets you up for financial success by knowing how much you need to save, how much you spend during your life, and ultimately, how to get to a retirement number you can be confident in when you retire. This is a lifestyle that, if followed properly, should help you attain financial success. What is financial success? I think it's being able to live your life financially comfortably so you can one day retire comfortably and enjoy retirement without having to worry about having enough money. How do you know you're on track to reach retirement? Let's take a look at some key milestones you should be reaching with your investments throughout your life.

Remember, from the ages of 20-60, you should hopefully be able to save and invest 15-25% of your net income. I understand that the ages of 20-40 are the years many people are trying to buy a home, get established, and start a family. There are many costs associated with doing all of these things. I understand you may need to pause up to 10% of your savings to save for a down payment or go towards paying on some personal debt to get paid off. From ages 20-40, you should be saving 15-25% of your net income. By the time you reach 40, you should have five times half of your pre-retirement net income. If your net income is $80,000, 50% of that is $40,000. You should have close to $200,000 in retirement savings in your core portfolio and other investment vehicles you have established. Hopefully, by the time you are 40 years old, your only debts should be a mortgage and/or a vehicle loan that should be paid off in three years or less if you follow the vehicle financing guidelines discussed in previous chapters. From the ages of 40-60, you should save 25% of your net income to go towards your retirement accounts. By the age of 50, you should be at 10 times half of your pre-retirement income. By the age of 60, you should be at 20 times half of your pre-retirement income. By the age of 60, your mortgage should be paid off, and you have a very clear picture of how much money you will need to live on minus the savings part of your budget and now minus the mortgage payment. From the ages of 60-65, here's where you should be utilizing that extra money you aren't paying on your mortgage and supercharge your savings going into retirement. You can add extra to your company-sponsored retirement, you can add to your other investment vehicles, and you can add extra to your emergency fund, which would be a good idea going into retirement. When you reach 65, you should now have 25 times half of your pre-retirement income in your retirement funds. These numbers should be very attainable for everyone who puts this budget into practice. If you averaged a market-like return of 7-8% over your lifetime, you should easily attain your retirement goals. Even if you underperformed historical market returns at 5%, using the rule of 72, your money would double in 14-15 years. The rule of 72 simply says if you take the rate of return and divide it into 72, that answer is how many years it takes for the money to double. At the age of 40, if you were to hit your target of five times half your pre-retirement income that was $200,000, at the age of 55, you should have close to $400,000 without even adding anything to it. If you had been adding a fourth of your net income to your retirement funds from the age of 40-55, then you would have an additional $300,000, not counting any growth. At 55, you should have at least $700,000 which would be 17.5 times your net income. Your target is to have 20 times by the age of 60. You are well on track in this illustration. I try not to get too hung up on investment returns when we discuss your retirement number because it's another variable you can't control. You can only go by historical returns. What if we go through a rough 20-year spell where market returns are below average? I think too much emphasis is placed on returns because it means you can tell everyone that if they only saved a little bit sooner, it could be much greater later. That's why I focus on how much you save and spend during your lifetime. If you make this a lifestyle, you are much more likely to achieve your retirement goals. I would rather count on my ability to control my savings and spending versus relying on my investment returns. I think one of the biggest problems with retirement calculators and other types of retirement income analysis is they try to overcompensate the lack of saving with projected market returns. I prefer to plan on returns as low as 4-5%, ensuring I will reach my retirement funding goals regardless of variables out of my control.

SOCIAL SECURITY BONUS

Something else I haven't discussed yet is social security. Why haven't I been discussing this part of your retirement income? Let's take a minute to discuss social security now. When constructing the *SHOW ME My Money Guide*, the idea was to eliminate as many variables as possible to help set you up for financial success. Social security was never designed to be your sole source of retirement income. It also seems to get quite a bit of scrutiny during different political cycles because they say we can't sustain it. While we are in the era of money printing, politicians could force central banks to print more money if needed. However, that may not be the case in the future. What if, during your working career, they extended the retirement age or reduced the amount you could draw on your social security? These are variables that cannot be accurately predicted by anyone. I believe the likelihood of any major changes is slim because whatever political party changes this for the worse, that individual or party will lose a lot of votes. I would rather look at it as a bonus instead of worrying about what they do with social security. That's right, a retirement bonus. You've done the hard work during your life, you've paid into it, and when it's time to retire, you can decide how much bonus you want and when you want it based on your wage history and the social security calculations. Right now, if you were born after 1960, your full retirement age is 67 years old. That's the age at which you can receive your full benefit. If you retire early at 62, you can get 70% of your social security benefit. If you wait until 70, you can get 130% of your benefit. There's a different percentage for each age in between those numbers. Those are the main ones people focus on. If you retire at 65, you may not want to draw your social security until 67 or 70 to get more of a benefit. Then again, you may have saved plenty for your retirement funds, and you want to start it at 62 because it would take 12 years to make that money back if you waited till 67. For those of you who are wondering about taking your social security early, that's the math. If you take it at 62, you get 70% of your benefit. If you wait until 67, you are waiting five years to draw anything. For those five years you waited, it would take 12 years to make up the difference versus 100% at 67. You would be 74 before you got back the full amount you received over those five years. There's a possibility you may not live that long. That's always something to consider when deciding to take your social security. If you waited until age 70 to take your retirement at 130% of the benefit, it wouldn't pay off until you were over 75 years of age. From that point on, you would be making more, but the question you have to ask yourself is how much longer is realistic. With advanced medicine, life expectancies continue to increase, and the quality of life for older people continues to improve. There's a good possibility you could live way past 75 years old. When you get to retirement, do you want to have to worry about whether or not you take it early or later? Do you want to have to depend on something that may or may not be there for you in the future? My answer to these questions is absolutely not. I would rather have the money saved myself in my retirement funds and look at social security as a bonus I can take now or wait to start. The benefit of social security is that it can help you preserve your retirement funds. If you've done the work on your budget, on saving and investing, and you know exactly what you spend, social security can be used to help keep more money in your retirement accounts. Use your social security to meet as much of your post-retirement expenses, then make up the difference with your retirement funds if you even need to. I would rather think of social security as a retirement bonus rather than a source of income.

SHOW ME CHEAT CODES

Who doesn't love cheat codes? I feel like this whole *SHOW ME My Money Guide* is a cheat code in itself. But I do have a few little cheat codes to help you make it even a little easier.

WORKING YEARS

During your working career, in your 20s to the age of 60, if you can save 25%, keep your housing under 30% and your vehicle loans under 10% of your net income, the rest is up to you how you spend it. If you can be disciplined on two-thirds of your spending, you have 35% to live on and spend however you want. This isn't hard to do as long as you set your savings and investing on auto-pilot each month and make sure your housing and vehicle loans are done the right way from the beginning. If you do that, you're on cruise control. All you have to do then is make sure the rest of your spending doesn't go over the remaining amount of your net income. That's easy.

POST-RETIREMENT

Once you retire, if you've set yourself on autopilot during your working career with your investments, you should no longer worry about how much to save. If you paid your mortgage off, there's a big chunk you no longer have to pay for each month. In retirement, all you have to spend money on is your Other Living Expenses and Some Housing costs, which should be 30% or less of your pre-retirement income. If you set up your retirement funds properly, you should have 50-60% of your pre-retirement income you can safely withdraw each year. Now, if you keep half of your money in retirement income for Necessities, the other half can be used for whatever you want. If you stick to the plan, half of your expenses are necessities; the other half can be whatever you want. This is an easy way for you to track everything each month.

EXTRA PAYROLLS / TAX REFUNDS / BONUSES

If you get your payroll check biweekly, or every two weeks, there are two months out of the year when you get three payrolls. Usually, that third payroll of the month does not have health insurance withheld, and possibly other pre-tax benefits you are having withheld from your paycheck, which means more money is going into your pocket on this payroll, too. When you do your budget, if you base your monthly net income on two payrolls, then you will have two months out of the year where you can use that extra money to your benefit. Since you don't rely on these two payrolls, you can take that extra money to pay down some high-interest debts, make your ROTH IRA contributions, replenish your emergency fund if needed, or invest in one of the other vehicles you have selected. If you get bonuses, you can apply this same concept when you get a bonus check. Another time you may get some extra money is during tax time. If you get a refund, use that money wisely. Use that extra money to help supercharge your savings or debt paydowns.

CONCLUSION

We have come to the end of the *SHOW ME My Money Guide* principles. I firmly believe that after you've read this book and implemented these principles, you will be equipped with the necessary tools to achieve financial success. I know we covered a multitude of financial topics and strategies. It may take several times reading through the book and several trial runs to build your budget. Once you have a handle on the principles and can get into a routine, you can master these principles. One day, after you've successfully reached your financial goals, people may come to you and say, "SHOW ME how you did it." You can tell them it was the *SHOW ME My Money Guide* that helped you reach your goals. Remember, finances are difficult to master. If you want to build your financial strengths, it takes time, practice, and discipline, much like diet and fitness. Keep practicing the principles and implementing them in your lifestyle and you can stay the course in the long run. It's also important for you to make sure and work with professionals like attorneys, CPAs, Insurance Agents, and Financial Advisors when needed for the expertise in the fields they serve. While implementing the strategies in this guide is reliant on your self-discipline, you must lean on the professionals when it comes to the areas of expertise they provide. Investment strategies mentioned in this guide are not a blanket endorsement but rather a guide to point you in the right direction. You are always welcome to do your own research and seek the advice of professionals to help you make your investment decisions. Additionally, any legal and tax information discussed in the guide is not to be considered advice. You should seek the help of an attorney or accountant if you need advice.

ABOUT THE AUTHOR

It can be difficult for clients to tell you what they really want from a financial standpoint. I believe my strength as a financial professional is my ability to solve financial problems for people by listening to their situation, empathizing with them, and creating the solution that best fits their needs.

I have been in the financial industry since 2009. I currently hold my series 7 and 66 licenses and have been a Certified Financial Planner™ since 2013. During college, I studied corporate Finance and Economics at Georgetown College in Kentucky, where I received my undergrad degree. I then followed that up with a master's in business administration a few years later.

I truly enjoy helping people better manage their finances, whether it's basic budgeting or complex tax issues. As a financial planner, I try not to make myself exclusive because I feel like if people are searching for financial help, someone needs to be there to help them. I have tried to build my practice around those needs, whether it's a young couple starting out, a small business owner trying to grow their business, or a retiree needing to prepare for post-career income.

Aside from being a financial professional, I try to spend as much time with my family as possible making fun memories. My hobbies include regularly exercising, healthy cooking, fishing, and doing whatever my two daughters are into at the time.

www.ingramcontent.com/pod-product-compliance
Lightning Source LLC
Chambersburg PA
CBHW071837210526
45479CB00001B/178